DAY B

CRUISING THE

THAMES

THOMAS BRUCE WHEELER

e.

COPYRIGHT

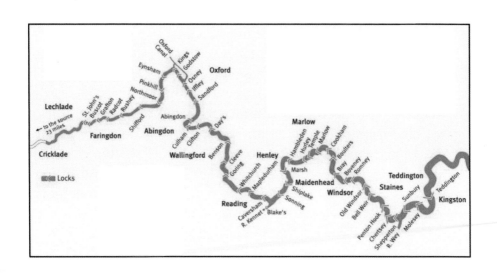

ABOUT THE AUTHOR

Thomas Bruce Wheeler is a retired Federal Senior Service Executive and Anglophile. In addition to his books on Sherlock Holmes, London, and cruising the Thames, Mr. Wheeler is curator of the Sherlock Holmes Collection on placingliterature.com. He is a graduate of the University of Missouri, with post graduate at the Darden Graduate School of Business (University of Virginia), and the Fuqua Graduate School of Business (Duke University).

Mr. Wheeler is a decorated military veteran, with an Infantry Silver Star for gallantry in action, and an Air Force Air Medal for the first 20 of his 26 combat missions. The Republic of Korea has also designated Mr. Wheeler an Ambassador for Peace. He is a member of Phi Kappa Psi, The English-Speaking Union, The Sherlock Holmes Society of London, and the Giant Rats of Sumatra.

At the bottom of Kris Cruisers web site's home page is a selection of *You Tube* videos. The one titled "*Kris Cruisers, Thames Holiday*" includes the author and his wife. They are the American couple who talk about their thirteen cruises.

FORWARD

For three decades my wife and I visited the UK once or twice a year. In this period we included over a dozen Thames River cruises. This book outlines the knowledge I gained, and presents it in a "how to" guide for those who have never cruised the Thames. If you want a convenient way to carry this information with you , the Kindle eBook version can be read on your smart phone.

In this paper book, some text is shown in red. These are the hyperlinks from the eBook. Hyperlinks transfer you to another place on the Internet, such as a restaurant's or town's web site.

One other word of caution, when friends hear you have taken others on a Thames cruise, they will want you to take them too. Thames cruises are like peanuts, you can not take just one.

.

                                                                    TBW

TABLE OF CONTENTS

PLANNING YOUR TRIP

Planning a Thames cruise involves four major tasks: assembling the "crew", selecting and reserving the boat, making airline reservations, and perhaps contacting a Cotswolds guide.

I recommend Kris Cruisers in Datchet as the marina from which to rent your boat. They are located just downstream from Windsor. The two cruisers I recommend are the 42 foot Lady Annalise which sleeps six, or the 48 foot Lady Elizabeth which sleeps eight (or ten in a pinch). Both are five star boats and have a lower lounge, full galley, an upper sun deck, and three heads/showers.

The larger Elizabeth is more expensive, but cheaper per couple. Cost and layouts are shown on Kris Cruisers' web page.

Another reason to rent a larger boat is that it provides more "deck hands". The Thames locks have full time British lock keepers, but each boat requires two linesmen, one in the front, and one in the rear, to secure the boat as water in the lock rises or lowers.

On when to plan your trip, I always preferred late May or early September, The weather is still good, and the boats have heaters for chilly mornings. In the Summer months the river is more crowded. Also, to avoid crowds, try to not select a week with a Monday bank holiday.

To get the boat and week you want, I suggest reserving a year in advance. This will also give you more time to find good airfares, and arrange your Cotswolds guide.

I always asked the marina to include two extra items on my boat, a small plastic stool with a short rope attached, and a chamois. The stool is for those mooring places where the step down to the dock is too high. The chamois is to wipe up the morning dew.

LADY ANNALISE

LADY ANNALISE

LADY ELIZABETH

The schedule I recommend in this book includes a free day on Tuesday for either a guided tour of the Cotswolds, or a visit to Oxford. You can use Google to find a Cotswolds guide. Find one that will meet you at the boat in Abingdon, and return you there at the end of the tour. You will not need a guide to see Oxford. You can use public transportation to get there, and then a local double-decker tour bus to see the town.

The final planning item you will have to deal with is the question: do I want to add additional days before or after the cruise? The train between Oxford/Datchet and London, originates at London's Waterloo Station

BEFORE YOU LEAVE HOME

There are a few things you should bring with you.

• A fold-up ice chest

• Binoculars. You will need them to see the river channel signs.

• A security wallet. The best way to share the cost of food and supplies is to have everyone donate to a common kitty, and pay for everything from it. This way you do not have to remember who paid for what.

• A rain suit for the driver. Although the boats both have inside driving positions, they are much easier to run from the top-side controls. If it rains, the driver will need a rain suit. **Before I bought a rain suit, I have made do with plastic leaf bags.**

• You will need a few British Pounds for a taxi when you arrive. You can buy Pounds from your bank at home, or ask friends who have been on a British trip. and have left over Pounds. In any case, do not buy too many. It is cheaper to use your credit cards to buy Pounds at British ATMs as you need them. There should be ATMs at Heathrow. For ATM withdrawals, make sure you have valid four digit pin numbers on at least two credit cards. **Call your credit card companies in advance, and tell them to expect charges from the UK.**

• Check with your health insurance company on your coverage overseas. You should consider travel insurance if you need coverage. Remember hats, sun blocker, sun glasses, and rain gear, It has been known to rain in Britain.

- The boats have built in sound and video systems, so if you have favorite music or movie CDs, bring them along.

- If you or a member of your crew has favorite games, bring them along too. You can not spend every evening in the pub. It is a bad idea to play cards for money, but for those who enjoy poker for fun, bring cards and chips.

- If you have a favorite hard liquor, you may be able to buy it duty free at your international airport. Wine and soft drink should be bought in Britain.

- Bring an old **unlocked** flip phone with you. In England you can buy a prepaid British sim card and convert your old phone to a British phone. Later in this book I will list the phone numbers of pubs, restaurants, etc. The phone will allow you to make reservations or call the Marina if you have a problem.

- On the boat, it is helpful to have 12 volt adaptors to charge your electronic devices. A 12 volt charger is the kind that fits into your car's cigarette lighter. They have 12 volt outlets on the boat.

- Onshore, the British electrical system in 220 volts, not the 110 volts we have in the U.S.. British electricity can destroy some U.S. equipment. Plan ahead and bring transformers and adaptor plugs to keep your devices safe. I have had good luck in finding what I needed on Ebay and Amazon.

- To gain the historical aspect of your Thames holiday, read *Three Men in a Boat* by Jerome K. Jerome.

ARRIVAL DAY

It is preferable if everyone arrives at London's Heathrow Airport, even if the flight to Gatwick is cheaper. Heathrow is just a six mile taxi ride from Kris Cruisers. Before you leave home, call the marina to find out how much the taxi should charge. At Heathrow, the taxi may not be metered, so make sure you have agreed on the price before getting in the car. By arriving at Heathrow Saturday morning, and beginning your cruise that afternoon, you avoid the expense of a hotel night.

If your crew is coming from different cities, I suggest you all meet at The Manor Hotel, in Datchet. You can have lunch there while the boat is being serviced. It is only a three minute walk to the marina. Have the taxi from Heathrow drop you and your luggage off at the marina, leave your luggage there, and walk to the hotel. This way you will not have to worry about later dragging your luggage to the boat. .

DATCHET

Ask the people in the hotel if there is a place in Datchet to buy the pre-paid sim card for your flip phone. If there isn't, you should be able to find a place in Windsor.

You should have bought British pounds with you, or purchased them at Heathrow. Now is the time to set up the "kitty". You will need it for provision shopping, lunch and dinner. Later in the cruise, when the kitty is flush and someone needs cash, they can charge a meal on their credit card and get reimbursed from the kitty.

After you check in at the marina's office. they will give you a tour of the boat. It is important that everyone pay attention. The boat has many pieces of equipment, and everyone should understand how to operate them. This ranges from checking the diesel engine to operating the head and galley equipment. The person selected to drive the boat will be given a quick shake-down cruise. Those who will become "linesmen" should also get instruction on how to throw the lines. The trick is to hold on to the loose end of the line in the hand that holds on to the boat's railing, and throw the looped line over the bollard posts. The lock keepers are very patient if you miss the first time or two.

KRIS CRUISERS MARINA

GENERAL INFORMATION

From mid-May to mid-September Thames River locks are manned between 9 a.m. and 6 p.m. Normally the locks are closed between 1 and 2 p.m. for the lock keeper's lunch. During the busy summer months, an assistant lock keepers may be hired to avoid the lunch-time closure.

Since the locks handle traffic going both ways, you may have to wait a few minutes for the lock keeper to motion you in. Make sure you keep your place in the queue. Entering the lock before your turn is bad form. During this period, most boats tie up on the shore. **However, since your boat has side thrusters, the trick I used when traveling upstream, was to lay off shore, with just enough power to offset the current. When the boat's bow starts to drift, a short burst from the side thruster will maintain the boat's static position.**

The side thrusters are also a good way to pull away from a dock. Think of a car parallel parked with cars close in front and back. If your car had a side thruster, it could swing the car's front end out from its tight spot.

Thames locks are large enough to handle two boats abreast. If you are the first boat in, you get your choice of which side. **Do not get too close to the lock's gate in front of you**. Your linesmen will throw lines over bollard posts to keep the boat secure. The linesmen should keep the lines taught, but adjust them as the water raises or lowers. **After the linesmen have secured the boat, turn off the engine.**

THAMES LOCK

LOCK WATCHERS

When cruising, keep near the center of the river and bear right when traffic approaches. Boats coming downstream have the right of way, as do sailboats and rowing skiffs. When you approach islands, there will be a direction arrow sign to show you the main channel. Sometimes branches may obscure the sign. This is why you brought binoculars.

Remember, you are in a cruiser, not a speedboat. Keep your speed to about 4 knots, the same as a brisk walking pace.

Since Kris Cruisers emptied your sewage tank before you left the marina, it should not require service during your week on the boat. If it does, stop at one of riverside marinas and have them handle the problem. Keep the receipt of what they charge. Kris Cruisers may reimburse you.

On the other hand, your fresh water tank requires regular attention. I suggest topping it off every chance you get. Some locks have hoses for this purpose. The more times you top off the tank, the less time it will take.

SATURDAY-DATCHET TO WINDSOR,

3 miles and 1 lock

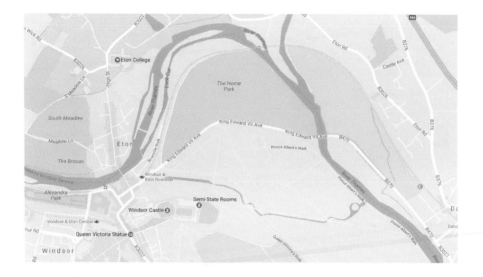

It will be afternoon before you leave the marina. You still have to stock the boat with food and supplies. I suggest shopping in nearby Windsor and then spending the night there to get over your jetlag. On the map above, the Datchet Marina is on the lower right corner, and at the lower left is my suggested mooring place at Alexandra Park in Windsor. As you approach the site, you will see the Cafe Barry on the shore.

WINDSOR MOORING PLACE

CAFE BARRY

The map below shows the location of the nearest Waitrose grocery store. After locking the boat, take the whole crew on the shopping trip. You will need them to carry the groceries, ice, drinks, wine etc. Many English grocery stores sell inexpensive cloth bags with handles. If you buy them here, they can be used throughout the cruise.

To get to the grocery store, walk east on Barry Avenue to Goswell Road. Walk south on Goswell under the railroad overpass. Then turn left on the path on the other side of the overpass. An elevator is at the end of the path. Take the elevator to the upper level. Then, turn n right on the pedestrian walkway to the grocery store.

On our cruises, we ate most breakfasts and some lunches on the boat, while having dinners and the other lunches in pubs and restaurants. The next two days will have longer cruises, and there will be no time for shore lunches, so shop accordingly. I suggest soup and ready-made sandwiches. Monday will be the next chance to resupply.

If you have not yet purchased a British sim card for your flip phone. you should be able to find one on nearby Peascod Street. Once installed, ask how you can add additional minutes by phone.

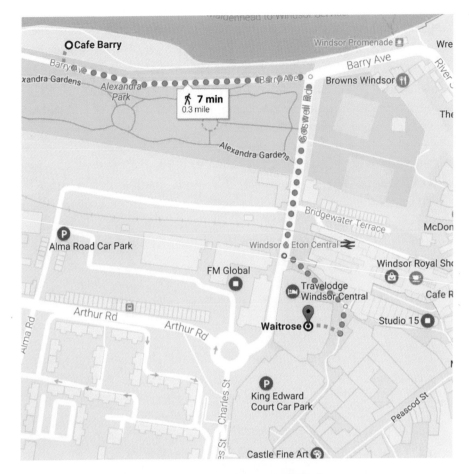

WINDSOR - GETTING PROVISIONS

After storing the provisions on the boat, you may want to walk to Windsor's Thames Street to see Windsor and find a place for dinner. There are pubs and restaurants galore. The easiest route to Thames Street is through the path by the Windsor & Eton Bowling Club. You walked pass it on your way to the grocery store.

While in Windsor, check what is playing at the Theatre Royal. You will be back in Windsor the following Friday, and may want to buy tickets for that evening.

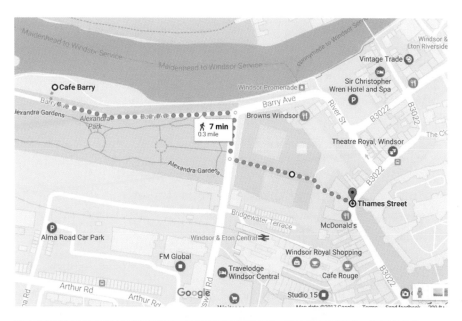

SUNDAY - WINDSOR TO SONNING, 26 miles and 10 locks

Sunday and Monday are two long cruising days. These are the days when you may have to eat lunch on the boat. I have recommended this schedule to allow a free day on Tuesday for either a day trip to the Cotswolds, or a visit to Oxford.

The first lock upstream from Windsor is Boveney. a little over 1 mile away. It opens at 9 a.m., so you may want to have breakfast and depart Windsor at 8:30 a.m.

On today's cruise you will also pass through Bray, Boulter's, Cookham, Marlow, Temple, Hurley, Hambleden, Marsh, Shiplake, and perhaps Sonning locks. **Stop at Shiplake Lock to top off your fresh water tank. If you can not see the water hose, ask the lock keeper.**

On your way to Sonning you will pass Marlow. West of the Marlow bridge, on the north side is the river is Higginson Park. This is the best place to moor on your way downstream next Thursday.

MARLOW, HIGGINSON PARK MOORING

Continuing upstream you will pass through Henley-on-Thames. Before you get to Henley, there is a long straight stretch in the river. This is the course for the famous Henley Regatta race. Temple Island is the starting point with the finish line at Henley.

After stopping to top off you fresh water tank at Shiplake Lock, you are just three miles from Sonning.

In Sonning, there are two places to moor. There is a small brick River bridge at Sonning. The first mooring place is just before the bridge. On your left is the Great House Hotel. There may be a mooring place where their lawn meets the river. If you tie up here, you should eat at least one meal in the hotel. I suggest a breakfast on their patio.

SONNING - THE GREAT HOUSE HOTEL

SONNING - UPSTREAM FROM THE LOCK

An alternative place to moor is upstream from the Sonning Lock. This place is on the river bank, and requires drive-in pegs to tie up the boat. Note the foot path on the far right side of the photo above.

Sonning is an attractive little village with a great country inn, The Bull. This is where I suggest you go for dinner. One note of warning, their portions are huge. Unless you have a large appetite, share.

If you moor above the Sonning Lock, follow the river path past the lock, and continue to the small path on your right that leads to the village church and The Bull.

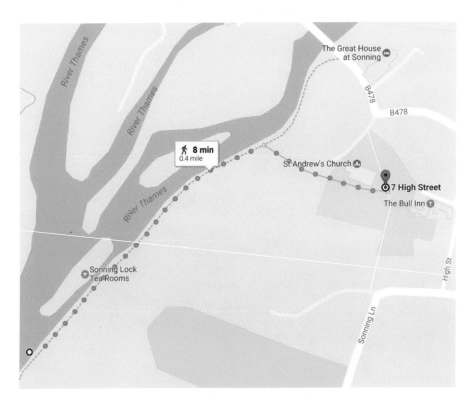

SONNING - TO THE BULL

SONNING - THE BULL

MONDAY - SONNING TO ABINGDON,
28 miles and 10 locks

This is another long day where it is appropriate to serve lunch on board. In addition, this is the day you will stop at a riverside Tesco to resupply your provisions.

Just two miles upstream from Sonning Lock is a large riverside Tesco Extra. Look for the wooden docks on your left, just pass the point where the Kennet Avon Cana l enters the Thames. Paths lead to the store, which is more like a Walmart than a grocery store. To save time, have your shopping list made out in advance. Have one person hold the main cart, while the shopping list is split up and given to multiple "shoppers". There is also an ATM outside the store to resupply your cash.

SONNING TO THE TESCO EXTRA

As you continue upstream you will pass through Caversham, Mapledurham, Whitechurch, Goring, Cleve, Benson, Days, Clifton, and Culham locks. Cleve Lock is where you will stop to top off your fresh water supply.

As you pass through Goring, before entering the lock, note the mooring places on your right. This may be the place you may spend Wednesday night. Beyond Goring Lock, between Goring and Wallingford, there are two upscale riverside restaurants, The Leatherne Bottel on the right, and The Beetle and Wedge on the left. In Wallingford I am partial to the pub grub at the 15th Century George Hotel on the High Street. In good weather, I enjoy eating in the their sheltered courtyard. Keep these places in mind for Wednesday's meals.

As you reach Abingdon, my suggested mooring place in on the right, just before the bridge. The spot is shown on the cover of this book. On the other side of the river is a marina where you can buy fresh water if you need it.

Warning: the river approaching Abingdon is shallow on the right side, keep in the center of the river until you are near the bridge, in the stretch shown below.

ABINGDON - NEAR THE BRIDGE

Abingdon is an attractive town, but does not have many good places to eat. I suggest two places for tonight's dinner, the Broad Face or the Crown & Thistle.. Both have recently been refurbished, and are located on Bridge Street. Just walk up to the bridge, cross the river, and you will see them on the right. You might want to try one tonight, and the other tomorrow night. I suggest you call ahead to book a table.

ABINGDON - THE BROADFACE

ABINGDON - THE CROWN & THISTLE

TUESDAY - COTSWOLDS GUIDED TOUR, OR VISIT OXFORD

As your crew planned their Thames holiday they should have decided if they wanted a guided tour of the Cotswolds, or a visit to Oxford. In either case, your hotel (boat) will remain in Abingdon.

If you selected the Cotswolds tour, you should have found your guide on the Internet. Arraign for him or her to pick you up in Abingdon. There is a nearby car park at which the guide can meet you. Give the guide your British cell phone number, so you can be called when he or she arrives. At the end of the tour, if your guide has done a good job, they will expect a tip

ABINGDON - CAR PARK NEAR THE BOAT

THE COTSWOLD

If you elect to visit Oxford on your own, the best way to get there is on public transportation. Once in Oxford, there are tour buses to show you the town. To get to the bus stop near your boat in Abingdon, walk across the bridge, past the Broad Face and the Crown and Thistle. On you left is the Abingdon County Hall Museum. On High Street, beyond the museum, is a bus stop. There, you can catch a red City Line bus to Oxford. The bus will be marked either X2 or X13. The trip is 33 miles and takes about 45 minutes. Ask about purchasing a return (round trip) ticket.

ABINGDON - COUNTY HALL MUSEUM

In Oxford, make sure to ask the bus driver where to board the return bus to Abingdon. I suggest lunch before exploring Oxford. There is an ancient pub called the Bear that I recommend.

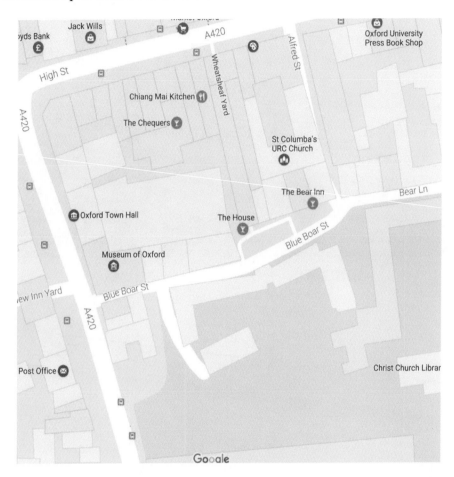

OXFORD - FINDING THE BEAR

OXFORD - THE BEAR

After lunch, walk up to Oxford's High Street, and ask where to catch the double-decker Oxford tour bus. If you get back to Abingdon in time, you may want to visit the Abingdon County Hall Museum. It is on the upper floor.

.

WEDNESDAY - ABINGDON TO GORING
- 19 miles and 6 lock

Today is the day when you will start cruising downstream. For lunch, I suggest the ancient George Hotel in Wallingford. There is also a new Waitrose grocery store just a block away to restock your provisions.

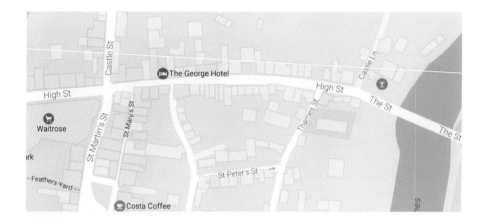

WALLINGFORD

WALLINGFORD - THE GEORGE

The place to tie up in Wallingford is just upstream from the bridge. There are usually several boats moored there, so space may be tight. It is much easier to dock the boat going against the current, in other words going upstream. I suggest you go under the bridge to find a place to turn around, and then approach the suggested mooring place going upstream. After lunch, it is only six miles to Goring, You can spend the night there, unless you have chosen to have a fancy dinner at the Beetle and Wedge, or the Leatherne Bottele. These require a call ahead for reservations, and permission to spend the night at their docks.

WALLINGFORD - MOORING

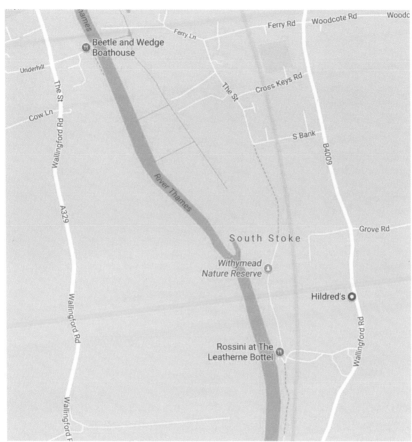

THAMES - BETWEEN WALLINGFORD AND GORING

GORING - MOORING

As I said, you have an option for dinner tonight, either the Beetle and Wedge, or the Leatherne Bottel, upstream from the Goring Lock, or a pub dinner in Goring. If you select the latter, I suggest the Catherine Wheel, The best way to reach the pub is to walk down stream on the Goring dock, across a little foot bridge, to an open field on your left. Walk through the field toward town. Then follow the streets on a six minute walk to the Catherine Wheel.

GORING - THE CATHERINE WHEEL

THURSDAY - GORING TO MARLOW, 25 miles and 9 locks

Today's cruise between Goring and Marlow might be another good day to have your lunch on board. Between Reading and Sonning, you will again pass the riverside Tesco Extra if you need to buy something.

The earlier you arrive at Marlow's Higginson Park, the better chance of getting a good mooring place. Marlow charges for mooring, so expect a visit from the fee collector.

MARLOW - HIGGINSON PARK MOORING

This might be a another good night to try something other than pub grub. Marlow has three good ethnic restaurants, the Tiger Garden for Indian cuisine, the Prince of Wales for Thai food, and the Villa D'Este, for an Italian dinner. You need to make reservations at these restaurants.

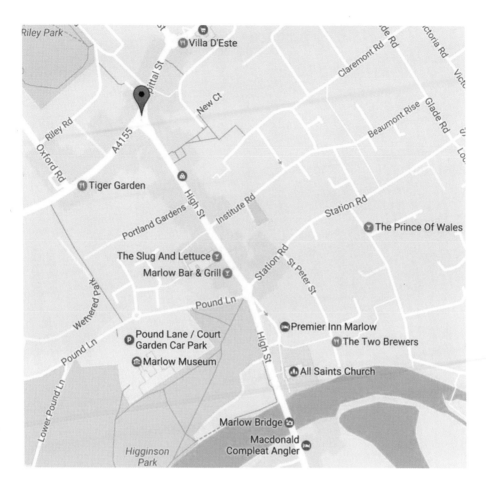

MARLOW - RESTAURANTS

MARLOW - THE PRINCE OF WALES

MARLOW - TIGER GARDEN

MARLOW - VILLA D'ESTA

Friday morning, before you leave Marlow, you might want to consider having a breakfast onshore. Marlow is the home of Burgers, a Swiss patisserie famous for pastries and English breakfasts. It is only a five minute walk from the boat.

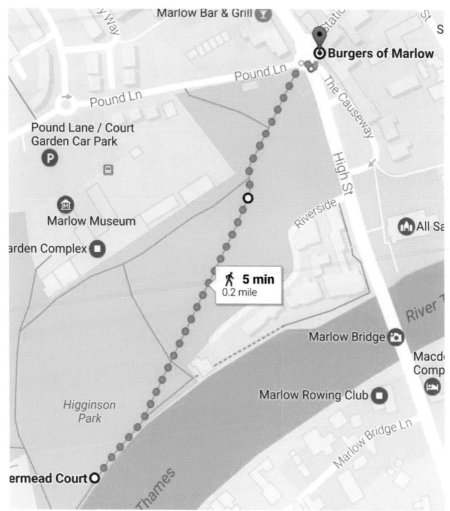

MARLOW - FROM THE BOAT TO BURGERS

MARLOW - BURGERS

FRIDAY - MARLOW **TO** DATCHET, **13**

miles and 6 locks

This short cruise is your last full day on the boat. I suggest cruising to Datchet where you can retrieve the luggage you left in the marina's locker. This will allow you to pack that evening. Before packing, take the train back to Oxford, and explore Oxford and Eton.

The previous Saturday, when you walked from the Manor House Hotel to the marina, you walked over railroad tracks. There is a little station on the east side of the street. This is where you catch the train to Oxford. This is also where those who are extending their holiday can take the train to London's Waterloo station. For those who want to visit Paris, you can board the Eurostar Chunnel train at London's Kings Cross Station. **If you elect to travel to London, buy your tickets at the** Windsor & Eton Riverside **train station in Windsor.**

SATURDAY - DEPARTURE DAY

Make sure you know what time on Saturday you must exit the boat. Those who are flying home from Heathrow can have the marina call them a taxi.

I hope you have enjoyed your week on the Thames as much as I have. Now is the time to start planning your next cruise.

Thomas Bruce Wheeler

TELEPHONE NUMBERS

44 is the British country code, and should only be used when calling the number from outside Britain. For a long distance call inside Britain, use the leading zero

DATCHET
Kris Cruisers   +44 (0) 1753 543930
The Manor Hotel   +44 (0) 1753 543442

WINDSOR
Waitrose Grocery Store   +44 (0) 1753 860565
Theatre Royal   +44 (0) 1753 853888
Windsor Riverside RR Station   +44 (0) 3456 000650

SONNING
The Great House Hotel   +44 (0) 1189 692277
The Bull Inn   +44 (0) 1189 693901
Tesco Extra   +44 (0) 3456 779573

ABINGDON
The Broad Face   +44 (0) 1235 538612
Crown & Thistle Hotel   +44 (0) 1235 522556
Abingdon County Hall Museum   +44 (0) 1235 522711
Oxford City Bus Company   +44 (0) 1865 785400.

OXFORD
The Bear Inn   +44 (0) 1865 728164
Oxford Tour Bus   **+44 (0) 1865 790522**

WALLINGFORD

The George Hotel +44 (0) 1491 836665
Waitrose Grocery Store +44 (0) 1491 832030
Beetle and Wedge +44 (0) 1492 651381
The Leatherne Bottel +44 (0) 1491 872667

GORING

The Catherine Wheel +44 (0) 1491 872379

MARLOW

Tiger Garden   +44 (0) 1628 482211
The Prince of Wales +44 (0) 1628 482970
The Villa D'Este +44 (0) 1628 472012
Burgers +44 (0) 1628 483389

BRITISH WORDS AND PHRASES

AFTERNOON TEA, or TEA, noun — England's traditional light refreshment, usually taken between four and six o'clock

ALL FOOL'S DAY, noun — April Fool's Day

AVOCADO PEAR, noun — avocado

BAD SHOW, noun — Contrary to accepted custom

BANGERS, noun — sausages

BANGERS AND MASH, noun — sausages and mashed potatoes

BANK HOLIDAY, noun — national holiday

BANK HOLIDAY WEEK, noun — the week in which the Monday Bank Holiday falls

BANK, THE, noun — the Bank of England

BARMAN, BARMAID, noun — bartender

BEDROOM WITH BATH ENSUITE, noun — bedroom with attached private bath

BEDSITTER (OR BEDSIT), noun — studio (one room) apartment

BEEF OLIVES, noun — a baked dish, made with thin slices of beef rolled around stuffing or vegetables,

BEEFEATER, noun (colloquial) — Warder in the Tower of London or Yeoman of the Guard, They find it mildly insulting to be called a Beefeater.

BEETROOT, noun — beet

BIG BEN, noun — the great clock bell in St. Stephan's Tower at the Houses of Parliament

BITTER, noun — a kind of draught beer

BLACK MARIA, noun — paddy wagon, police van

BLACK OR WHITE?, adjective - "Do you want black coffee or with cream?"

BLEEDING, adjecti

BLIGHTER, noun (slang) — contemptuous term for an obnoxious or annoying person

BLOKE, noun — guy, fellow, man

BLOODY, adjective, adverb ve, adverb — vulgar euphemism for the now overworked swear word "bloody" — expletive, swear word, now accepted and overworked

BLOOMING, adjective (slang) - damned, euphemism for bloody

BOG, noun (slang) — toilet

BOILED SWEETS, noun — hard candy

BONNET, noun — engine hood on a motor vehicle

BOOT, noun — trunk (of an automobile)

BOWLER (HAT), noun — derby

BRACES, noun — suspenders

BRAKE, noun — station wagon (automobile)

BUCK HOUSE, noun (colloquial) — Buckingham Palace

BUM, noun (slang) — buttocks

BUNS, noun — small sweet rolls

BUTTERY, noun — formerly the cool room in a large medieval house where the beer was kept, now a university snack bar or café

CAF, noun (slang) (abbreviation) — café, restaurant

CHAP, noun (colloquial) — man, fellow

CHAPEL, noun — church for any Christian religion

CHEEK, noun, verb (colloquial) — nerve; to be impudent

CHEMIST (SHOP), noun — druggist, drug store

CHIN-CHIN, exclamation — a word used in greeting and farewell, and in a toast (from the Chinese Dqingqing)

CHIPS, noun - French fried potatoes

CITY, THE, noun — the old part of London, the financial district

CLOTTED CREAM, noun — milk thickened by scalding, a part of desserts, e.g. clotted cream and strawberries

CLUBLAND, noun — an area, such as St. James's in London, where the private clubs are located

COACH, noun — bus

COTTON, noun - thread — "Here, I have a needle and cotton; I can now sew on that button."

COTTON REEL, noun — spool of thread

COTTON WOOL, noun — absorbent cotton ball

COUNCIL ESTATES, noun—public housing

CREDIT ACCOUNT, noun—charge account

CRISPS, noun—potato chips

DAME, noun—title for a woman, corresponding to a knighthood for a man

DEMARARA, noun—raw brown sugar

DIARY, POCKET, noun—notebook

DOMESDAY BOOK, noun (historical)—A census record of England ordered by William the Conqueror in the 11th-Century.

DOUBLE CREAM, noun—whipping cream

DOUBLE FIRST, noun—a person who has won first class honors in two college majors

DUKE, noun—a nobleman of the highest rank next to a prince, (A Royal Duke is also a prince.)

EARL, noun—a nobleman ranking below a marquis, but above a viscount

EGG-FLIP, noun—eggnog

ESTATE AGENT, noun—real estate agent

EX- DIRECTORY (Telephone), noun—unlisted number

FLANNEL, noun—washcloth

FAIRY CAKE, noun—cup cake

FANNY, noun (vulgar slang)—female genitals

FATHER CHRISTMAS, noun—Santa Claus

FEN, noun — marsh, boggy land

FIRE BRIGADE, noun — fire department

FIRST FLOOR, noun — the floor above the ground floor, i.e. the second floor

FISH FINGERS, noun — fish sticks

FISHMONGER, noun — dealer in fresh fish

FIVER, noun — five pound note

FLAG DAY, noun — fund-raising as in the United States on Poppy Day

FLAT, noun — one floor apartment

FOOTBALL, noun — soccer

PAVEMENT, noun — sidewalk

FORM, noun — grade or class at school

FORTNIGHT, noun — two weeks

FRENCH BEAN, noun — string bean

FRIED BREAD, noun — bread fried in bacon grease

FRUIT MACHINE, noun — slot machine

GENTS', noun (colloquial) — men's toilet

GET KNOTTED, exclamation (slang) – "go to the Devil!"

GET UP ONE'S NOSE, verb (colloquial) — to irritate or annoy one

GREEN GROCER, noun — a dealer in fresh vegetables and fruit

GROUND FLOOR, noun — first floor

GUINEA, noun — twenty-one shillings in old currency, now the equivalent of one pound, five pence

GUM BOOTS, noun — rubber boots

HAGGIS, noun (Scotland) — traditional dish made of sheep organs, ground with suet, oatmeal and seasoning, boiled in a sheep's stomach

HARLEY STREET, noun — the London Street where eminent physicians and surgeons have their offices, the term is now a by-word for upscale medical specialists

HIGH TEA, noun — a substantial early evening meal, usually in lieu of supper

HOOVER, HOOVERING, noun & verb — vacuum cleaner, vacuuming

HUNTING PINK (PINKS), noun — the scarlet coat worn by men in the foxhunt

IN THE CLUB, prepositional phrase (slang) — pregnant

INGLENOOK, noun — ancient "walk-in" fireplace

INSIDE LEG, noun — inseam trouser measurement

JACKET POTATO, noun — baked potato

JUMBLE SALE, noun — "rummage" sale, usually as a benefit for a church or school

JUMPER, noun — a pull over sweater

KNICKERS, noun — women's panties

KNOCK UP, verb — to rouse or waken someone

LAGER, noun — pale beer, like the popular beers served in North America

LEMON SQUASH, noun — lemonade

LIFT, noun — elevator

LITTER BIN, noun — wastebasket

LIVERY COMPANY, noun — one of The City's (London) Companies that had distinctive costumes

LOCAL, THE, noun (colloquial) — the neighborhood pub

LONG-CASE CLOCK, noun — grandfather clock

LOO, noun (colloquial) - toilet — Said to be from the French chambermaids who cried "gardez l'eau!" before emptying the chamber pots from upstairs windows.

LORD, noun — Peer of the Realm, or a person given the title by courtesy

LORRY, noun — truck

LOST PROPERTY, noun — lost and found department

LOUNGE SUIT, noun — business suit

LUGGAGE, noun — baggage

MACINTOSH, MACKINTOSH, MACK, noun — a raincoat

MATE, noun (colloquial) — friend, co-worker

MEAN, adjective — cheap, as in cheapskate

MICHAELMAS, noun — Feast of St. Michael, every September 29

MINI-CAB, noun – a taxi available only if ordered in advance, and not permitted to cruise for fares

MOOR, noun — open land

MOTOR, MOTOR CAR, noun — car, automobile

MOTORWAY, noun — freeway, similar to U.S. Interstate Highways

NAIL VARNISH, noun — fingernail polish

NANNY, noun — a child's nurse (not a medical nurse)

NAPPIE, noun — baby's diaper

NEWSAGENT, noun — shop selling newspapers, candy, tobacco, etc

NOTE, noun — paper money, e.g., five pound note

NOTECASE, noun — wallet, billfold

OLD BAILEY, noun — nickname for London's Central Criminal Court located on Old Bailey Street.

OLD BOY, noun — former pupil of a school

OPERATING THEATRE, noun — operating room in a hospital

PANTO, noun (abbreviated colloquialism) — pantomime, Pantos are traditional Christmas shows, to which children are taken.

PARSON'S NOSE (also POPE'S NOSE), noun — tail of a cooked fowl

PAST IT, verb — getting too old for one's job

PEPPER POT, noun — peppershaker

PERPENDICULAR (ENGLISH PERPENDICULAR), noun —
15th to 16th- century English Gothic architecture

PETROL, noun — gasoline

PICKLED CUCUMBERS, noun — pickles

PISS-OFF, verb (vulgar) — go away, beat it

PLIMSOLLS, noun — tennis shoes

PLONK, noun (colloquial) — a cheap wine

POLLING DAY, noun — Election Day

POOF, noun (slang, derogatory) — a male homosexual

POSH, adjective — elegant, luxurious — some say this is an acronym from the Empire days when the shady side of the ship was preferable when going to and from India, hence, "Port Out, Starboard Home".

POST, noun — mail

POSTMAN, noun — mailman

POSTWOMAN, noun — a female letter carrier

POTATO CRISPS, noun — potato chips

PUB, noun (abbreviation, colloquialism) — public house, bar, inn

PUBLIC SCHOOL, noun — private school

PUDDING CLUB, noun - pregnant, (usually "in the pudding club")

PUT DOWN, verb — to kill an animal to prevent suffering

QUARTER DAY, noun — day on which payments are due for the preceding three months — In England the four quarter days are: Lady Day, Midsummer Day, Michaelmas, and Christmas.

QUEER STREET, noun — to be in Queer Street is to be in trouble, especially financial difficulty

QUEUE, QUEUE UP, verb — line up, wait in line — Queuing is the custom in London, and failure to take one's proper place in line is a serious breach of etiquette.

REDUNDANT, adjective — to be made redundant is to be laid off from one's work

RETURN TICKET, noun — round trip ticket

RING, RING UP, verb — call on the telephone

RISING DAMP, noun — increase in moisture in the walls of a structure

ROYAL, noun — a member of the Royal Family

ROYAL DUKE, noun — hereditary title for a male member of the Royal Family, especially the son(s) of the reigning monarch

ROYAL WARRANT, noun — commission recognizing a tradesman who supplies goods to a royal person

RUBBER, noun — eraser

RUDE PARTS, noun — the genitals

SCHOOL TIE, noun — a distinctive necktie worn by graduates of specific schools, or members of clubs or regiments

SCONE, noun — a sweet biscuit of barley-meal, oatmeal or wheat flour, baked in an oven or on a griddle, usually made with raisins

SERVIETTE, noun — table napkin

SHILLING, noun — former monetary coin that was worth 1/20 of a pound or 5 pence

SHOP GAZING, verb (colloquial) — window shopping

SINGLET, noun — man's T-Shirt

SISTER, noun — title of a senior nurse in a hospital ward or department — also, colloquially, any female nurse

SLEEPING ROUGH, verb — sleeping outdoors

SORBET, noun — sherbet

SPEND A PENNY, euphemism — go to the bathroom

SPOTTED DICK, noun (slang) — plum duff, plain flour pudding with raisins or currants

SQUIRE, noun — a country gentleman, especially the district's chief landowner

STALLS, noun - theater seats in the lower area near the stage

STERLING, noun — British money, as in Pound Sterling

STICKY WICKET, noun (figurative) — a difficult or delicate situation - from trying to play cricket on a muddy field

STREAKED RASHERS, noun — American style bacon strips

SUGAR BASIN, noun — sugar bowl

SURGERY, noun—consulting office of a dentist or general medical practitioner

RING, RING UP, verb—call on the telephone

RISING DAMP, noun—increase in moisture in the walls of a structure

ROYAL, noun—a member of the Royal Family

ROYAL DUKE, noun—hereditary title for a male member of the Royal Family, especially the son(s) of the reigning monarch

ROYAL WARRANT, noun—commission recognizing a tradesman who supplies goods to a royal person

RUBBER, noun—eraser

RUDE PARTS, noun—the genitals

SCHOOL TIE, noun—a distinctive necktie worn by graduates of specific schools, or members of clubs or regiments

SCONE, noun—a sweet biscuit of barley-meal, oatmeal or wheat flour, baked in an oven or on a griddle, usually made with raisins

SERVIETTE, noun—table napkin

SHILLING, noun—former monetary coin that was worth 1/20 of a pound or 5 pence

SHOP GAZING, verb (colloquial)—window shopping

SINGLET, noun—man's T-Shirt

SISTER, noun—title of a senior nurse in a hospital ward or department—also, colloquially, any female nurse

SLEEPING ROUGH, verb—sleeping outdoors

SORBET, noun—sherbet

SPEND A PENNY, euphemism—go to the bathroom

SPOTTED DICK, noun (slang)—plum duff, plain flour pudding with raisins or currants

SQUIRE, noun—a country gentleman, especially the district's chief landowner

STALLS, noun - theater seats in the lower area near the stage

STERLING, noun—British money, as in Pound Sterling

STICKY WICKET, noun (figurative)—a difficult or delicate situation - from trying to play cricket on a muddy field

STREAKED RASHERS, noun—American style bacon strips

SUGAR BASIN, noun—sugar bowl

SURGERY, noun—consulting office of a dentist or general medical practitioner

SWAN-UPPING, verb—the annual capturing and tagging of Thames swans

SWISS BUN, noun—Danish coffee roll

TEA CAKE, noun—a light, flat sweet bun, eaten at teatime

TELLY, noun (colloquial)—television or television set

TOAD IN THE HOLE, noun—sausages, fried, then baked in batter

TROTTERS, noun (slang)--pig's feet

TRUNK CALL, noun—long distance telephone call

V.A.T., noun – acronym for Value Added Tax, a national sales tax that is added to the price paid by purchasers.

VERGE, noun — shoulder (of a road)

VEST, noun — man's undershirt

WAISTCOAT, noun — vest

WELLIES, WELLINGTONS, noun — rubber boots, usually knee-high

WEST END, noun--the fashionable district of London, including Piccadilly, Mayfair and St. James's

Y-FRONT, noun — jockey style men's underwear

ZEBRA CROSSING, noun — pedestrian street-crossing, named for the pavement stripes

BOOKS BY THOMAS BRUCE WHEELER-

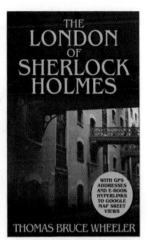

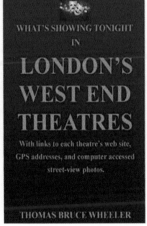

Gate 5 Penton Hook Marina
Staines Rd.
Chertsey
   Surrey KT 16
      8 PY .
United Kingdom

Printed in Great Britain
by Amazon